Movie Heroes for Students

C000110995

10 Graded Selections for Early Intermediate Pianists

Arranged by
Tom Gerou

Some of the most memorable movie themes come from action and adventure films. This collection contains 10 very popular themes that are frequently requested by students of all ages. *Movie Heroes for Students*, Book 2, is arranged at the early-intermediate level. Sixteenth notes and triplets have been avoided. Key signatures are limited to one sharp or flat. Chords contain a maximum of three notes in either hand and simple meters of $\frac{4}{4}$ or $\frac{3}{4}$ allow for greater accessibility.

Alfred Music Publishing Co., Inc.
P.O. Box 10003
Van Nuys, CA 91410-0003
alfred.com

ISBN-10: 0-7390-8030-X
ISBN-13: 978-0-7390-8030-6

Batman Theme

Words and Music by Neal Hefti
Arr. by Tom Gerou

With a steady, driving beat

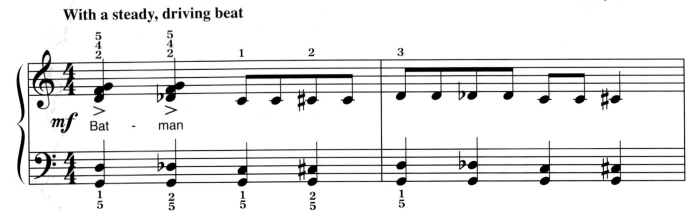

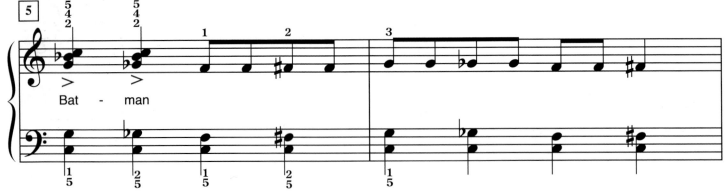

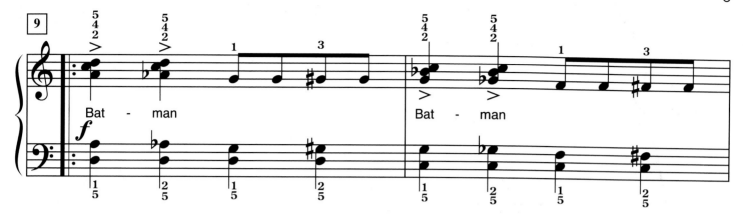

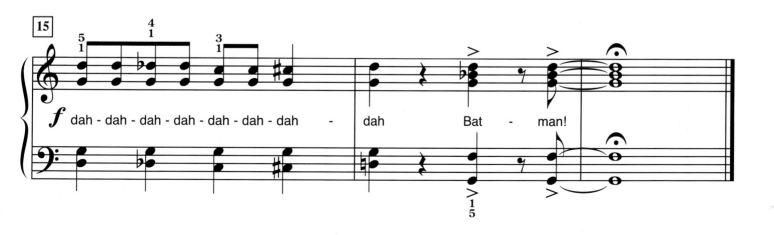

Hedwig's Theme

from *Harry Potter and the Sorcerer's Stone*

Music by **JOHN WILLIAMS**

Arr. by Tom Gerou

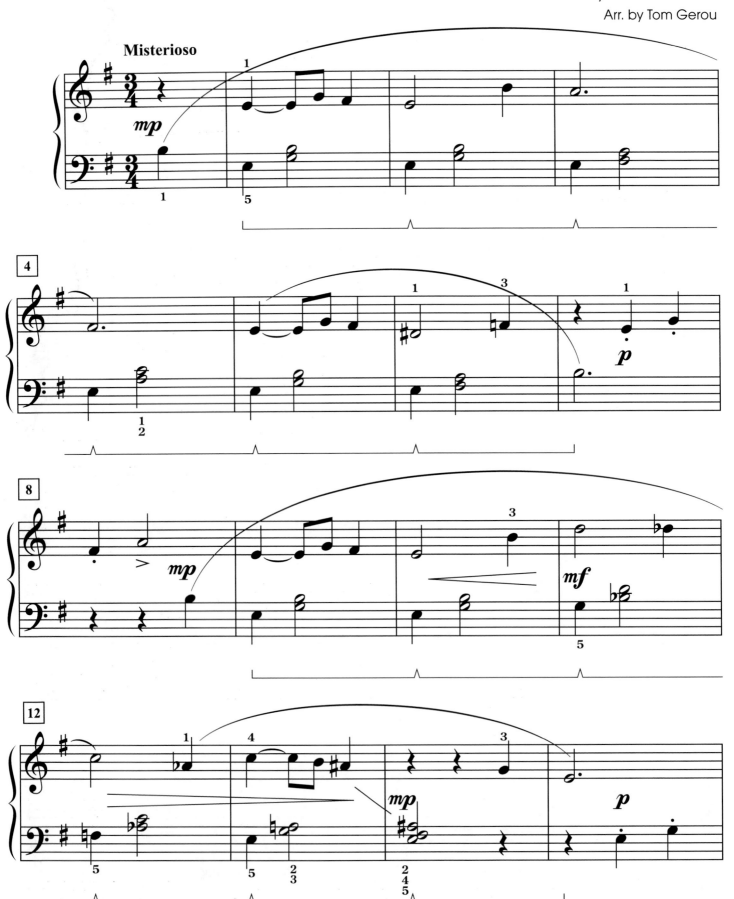

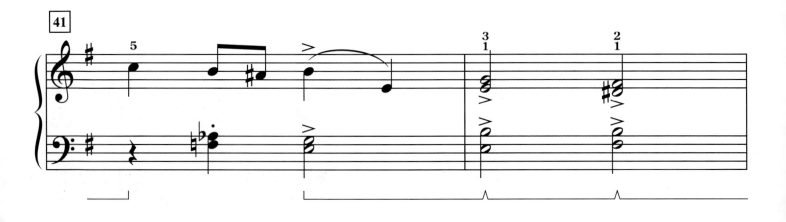

Iron Man

Words and Music by
Frank Iommi, John Osbourne,
William Ward and Terence Butler

Arr. by Tom Gerou

Moderately slow

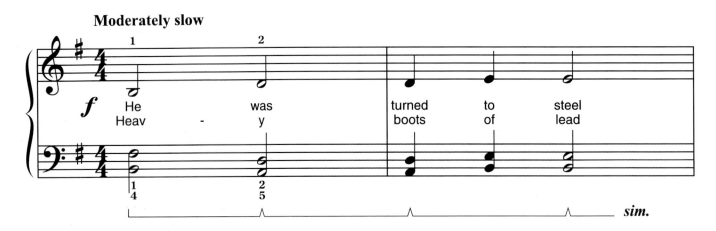

He was turned to steel
Heav - y boots of lead

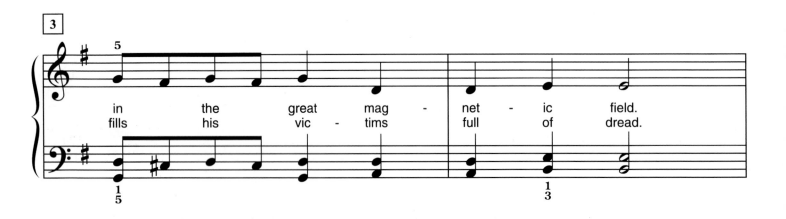

in the great mag - net - ic field.
fills his vic - tims full of dread.

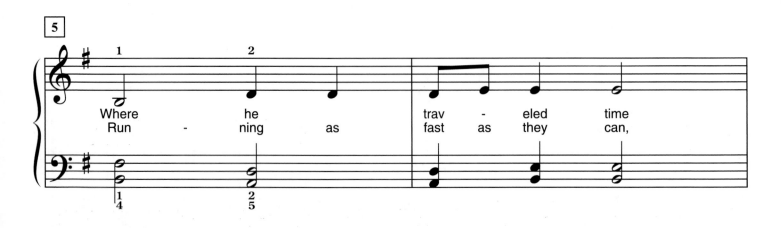

Where he trav - eled time
Run - ning as fast as they can,

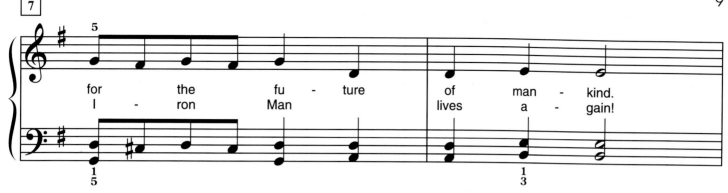

for the fu - ture of mankind.
I - ron Man lives a - gain!

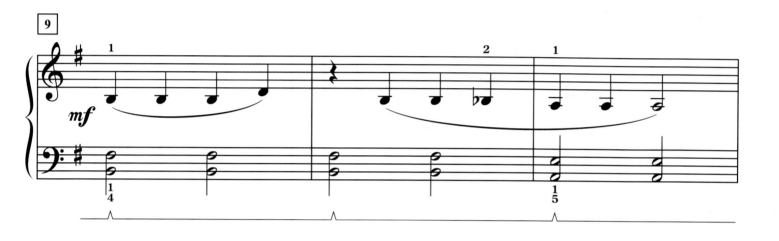

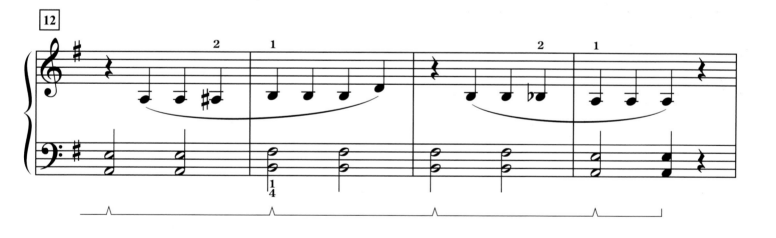

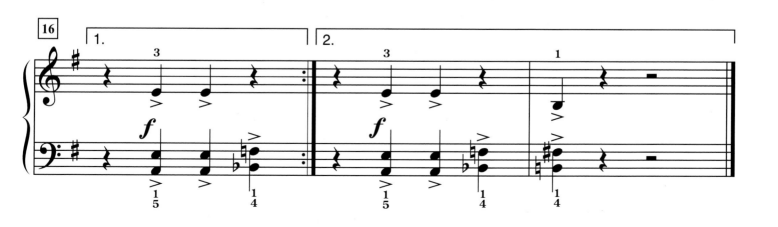

He's a Pirate

from Walt Disney's *Pirates of the Caribbean: The Curse of the Black Pearl*

By Klaus Badelt

Arr. by Tom Gerou

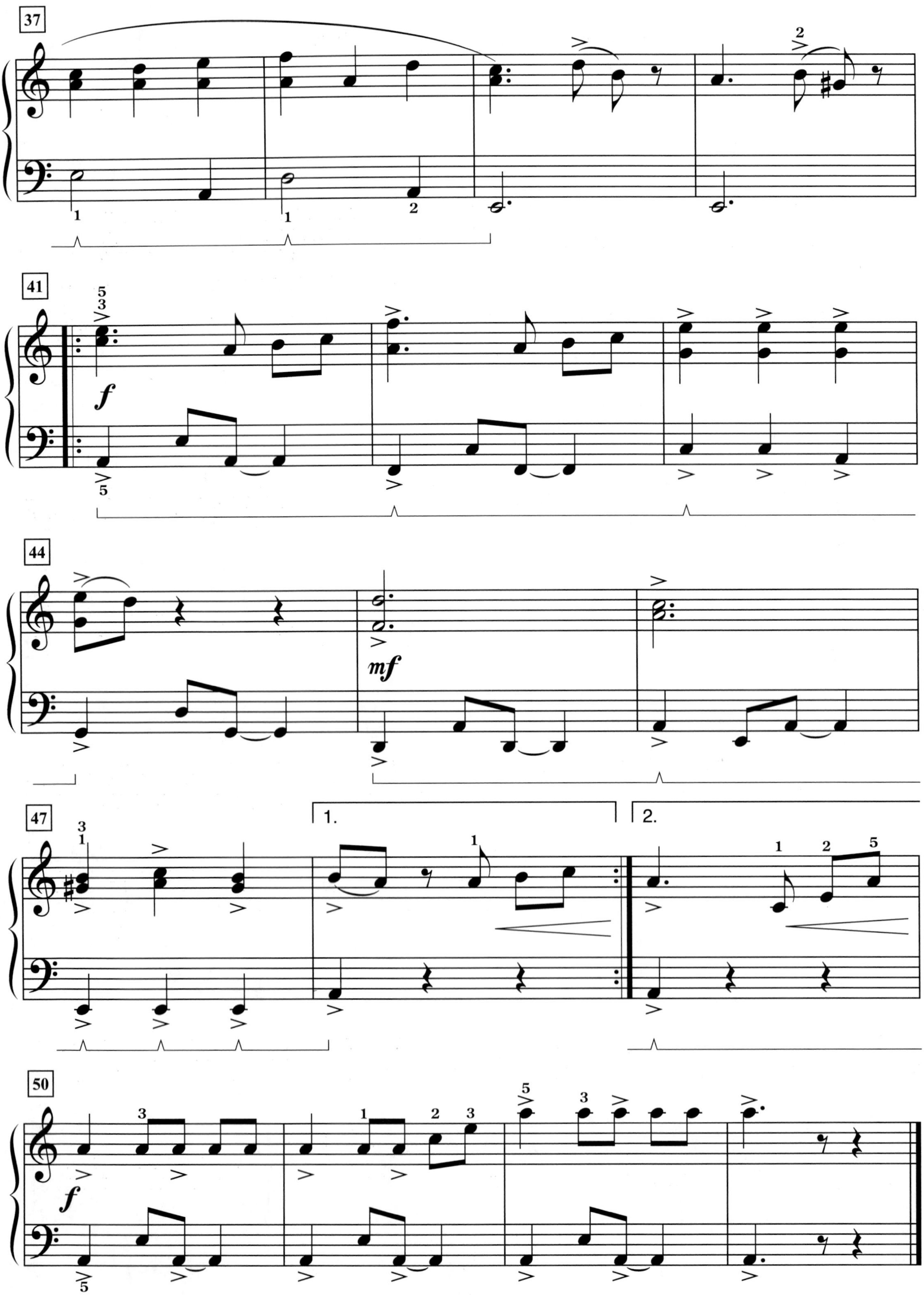
37
41
f
44
mf
47
1.
2.
50
f

James Bond Theme

By Monty Norman
Arr. by Tom Gerou

Princess Leia's Theme

from *Star Wars*

Music by **JOHN WILLIAMS**

Arr. by Tom Gerou

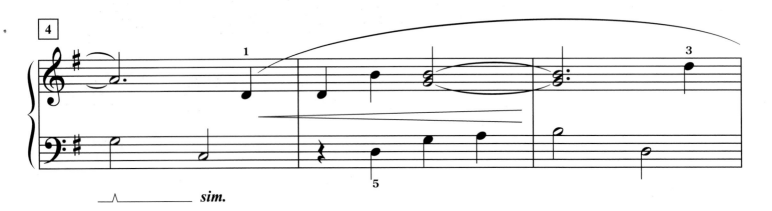

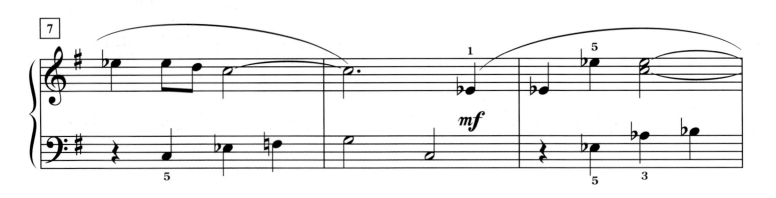

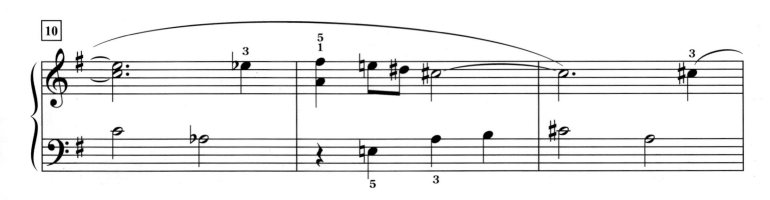

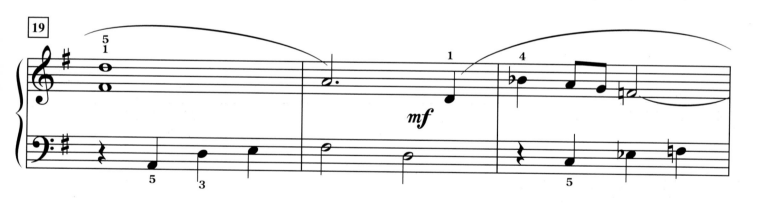

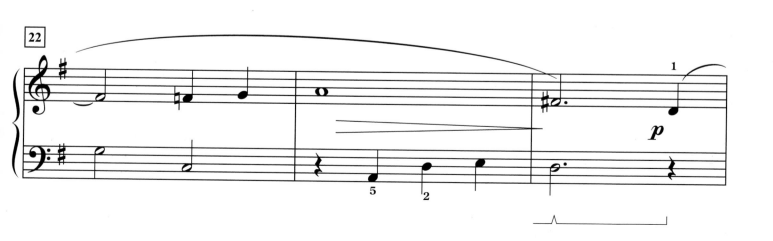

Raiders March

from *Raiders of the Lost Ark*

Music by **JOHN WILLIAMS**
Arr. by Tom Gerou

March

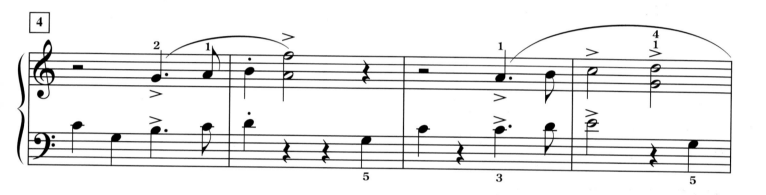

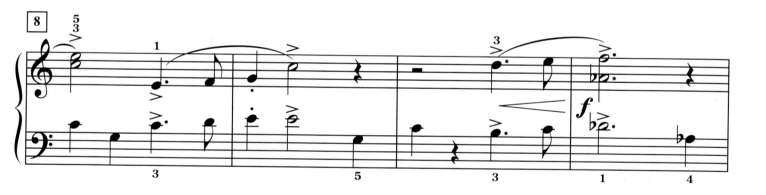

20

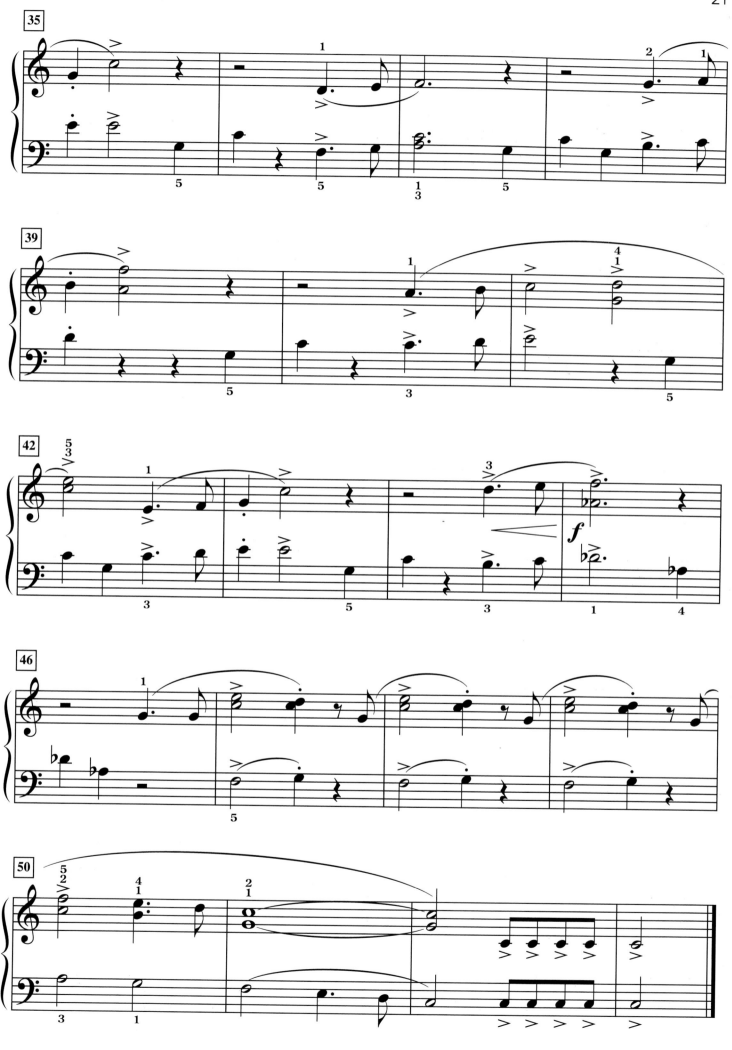

Star Wars
(Main Theme)

Music by **JOHN WILLIAMS**
Arr. by Tom Gerou

Theme from *Superman*

Music by **JOHN WILLIAMS**

Arr. by Tom Gerou

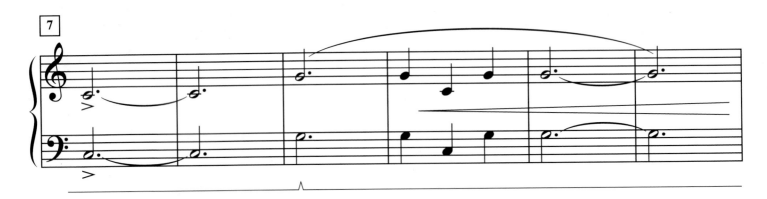

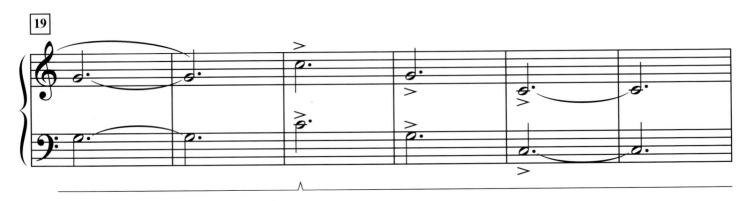

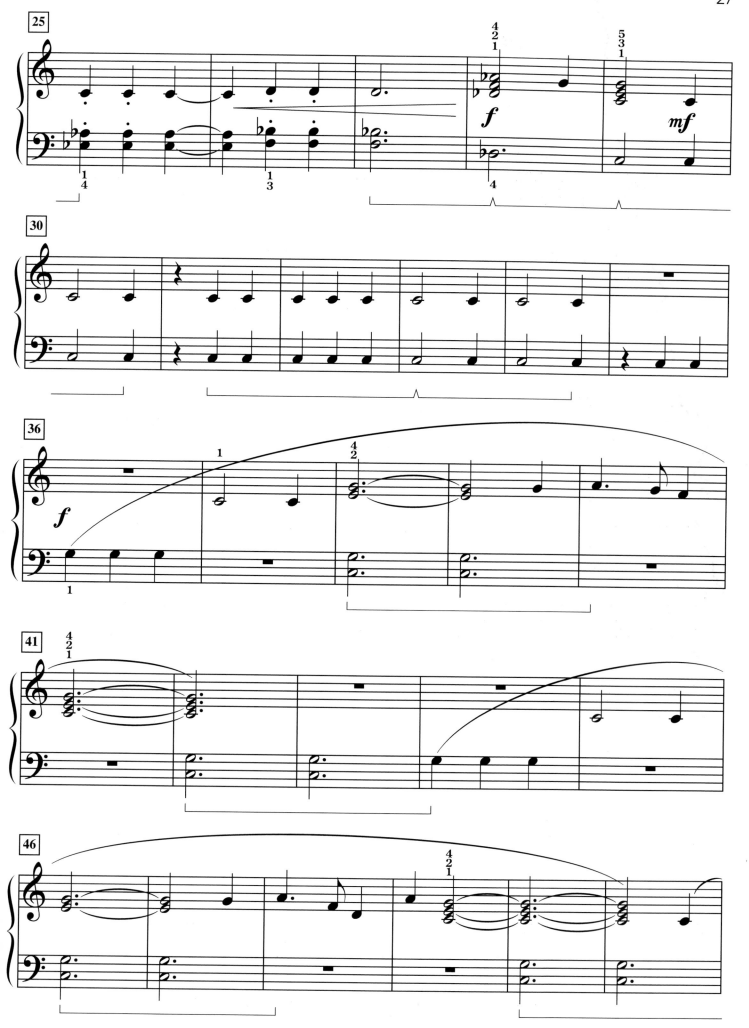

28

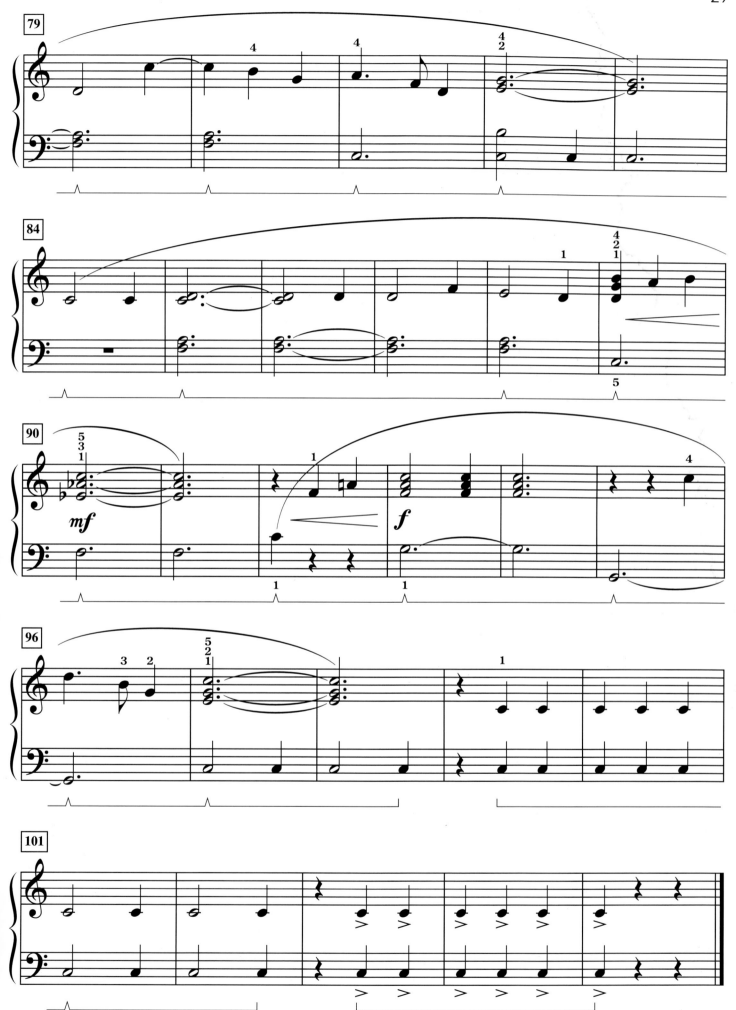

Wonder Woman

Words and Music by
Norman Gimbel and Charles Fox
Arr. by Tom Gerou

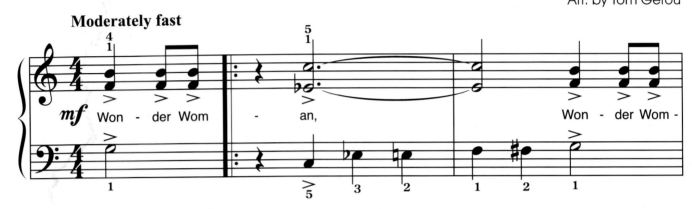

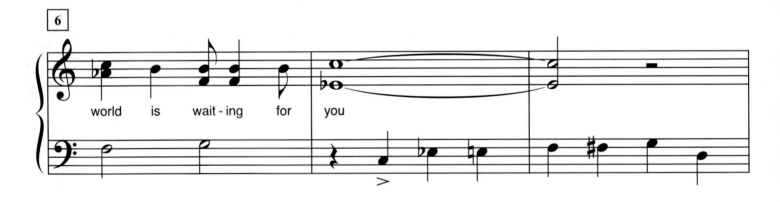

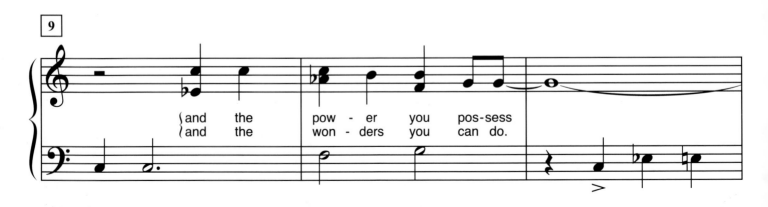

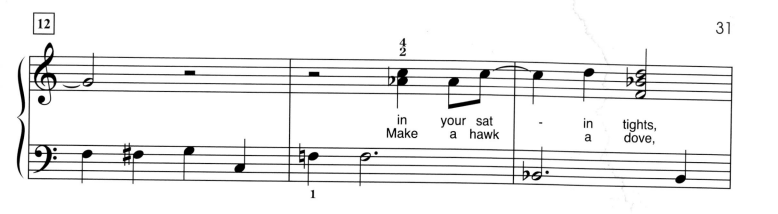

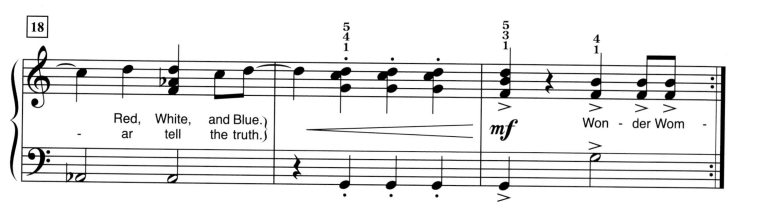